THE ART OF
SELF CULTIVATION
Quotations from Chinese Wisdom

Copyright © 2012 Shanghai Press and Publishing Development Co., Ltd.

All rights reserved. Unauthorized reproduction, in any manner, is prohibited.

This book is edited and designed by the Editorial Committee of *Cultural China* series.

Managing Directors: Wang Youbu, Xu Naiqing
Executive Editor: Yang Xinci
Editor (Chinese): Zhang Wei
Editors (English): Zhang Yicong, Yang Xiaohe

Compiled by Yang Tianwen
Translated with notes by Tony Blishen

Design Consultant: Diane Davies
Designer: Wang Wei
Cover Image: Getty Images

ISBN: 978-1-60220-133-0

Address any comments about *The Art of Self Cultivation* to:

Better Link Press
99 Park Ave
New York, NY 10016
USA

or

Shanghai Press and Publishing Development Co., Ltd.
F 7 Donghu Road, Shanghai, China (200031)
Email: comments_betterlinkpress@hotmail.com

Printed in China by Shenzhen Donnelley Printing Co., Ltd.

3   5   7   9   10   8   6   4

THE ART OF
SELF CULTIVATION
Quotations from Chinese Wisdom

COMPILED BY YANG TIANWEN
TRANSLATED WITH NOTES BY TONY BLISHEN

Better Link Press

Contents

Foreword

This is the first of a two volume collection of quotations covering two aspects of Chinese thought as it concerns human behavior. The quotations are drawn not only from the works of well known early philosophers such as Kongzi (Confucius), Meng Ke (Mencius) and Li Er (Laozi), but also from other texts and include a range of commentators who wrote as late as the 17th, 18th, and 19th centuries. The time span is thus one of over two thousand years, starting in approximately 500 BC, and is more or less equivalent to the time span occupied in the history of western thought by Plato, born in 428 BC at one end, and say, Rousseau born in 1712, at the other.

The views of the individual and society presented through these quotations are the views of a highly literate elite. From very early on, the Chinese imperial examination system for entry to government service emphasized literary scholarship, so that every senior official was a scholar first and an administrator second and almost by definition a poet as well. There was, thus, a tendency to see the world as one of the literate rulers and the less literate ruled, where it was the function of the ruler to secure the well-being of the ruled, though that was not always the case. It was a world also, where, generally, custom and principle were more important than religious faith. Almost all the quotations are drawn from the writings of men who were, at some time in their lives, officials of one sort or another, as members of a central bureaucracy, or as provincial or district administrators and magistrates.

This first volume comprises quotations which concern themselves with what in Chinese is termed *xiushen* which translates roughly as "self cultivation." One Chinese encyclopedia defines it as "the nurture of body and mind in order to strengthen and raise the level of one's sense of morality." *Xiushen* addresses individual behavior and conduct from the essentials of character such as morality, through activities like the acquisition of knowledge and the techniques of learning to the norms of correct social behavior. Mencius, for one, believed that an individual's moral sense had applications beyond the realms of personal behavior and that the qualities of the morally complete person could "bring peace to all under heaven."

Most of the major philosophical texts from which many of these quotations are drawn were translated into English during the 19th century by

James Legge, the Scottish missionary and from 1876, the first professor of Chinese at Oxford University. Legge's translations comprised six volumes of the monumental 50 volume series *Sacred Books of the East* of which he was joint editor. Although Legge and his assistant Wang Tao started work on his translations in 1841, the first was not published until 1879 and the last in 1891. Legge's translations included *The Confucian Analects*, the *Classic of History*, the *Classic of Poetry*, the *Record of Rites* as well as the *Classic of Morality* and other Daoist texts.

The task of the translator today is less onerous than that which confronted Legge over 150 years ago. Although the classical Chinese language is often terse to the point of obscurity, there are now electronically accessible modern Chinese glosses of the original texts and other tools which ease the task of translation considerably. Even so, there are often multiple interpretations of obscure texts and disputes over their significance, which have run for centuries. Chinese scholarship was very much one of literary exegesis.

This book would not have been possible before the advent and development of the internet since the task of consulting sources and assembling text would have been so laborious and time-consuming as to be self-defeating. It is, however, a book of compilation rather than scholarship and is intended for the general reader rather than the specialist. By the same token, notes which describe the source of each quotation have been placed at the end of each volume, both to give a glimpse of the realities of the time and to illustrate the kind of personalities, some of them engagingly eccentric, who recorded their thoughts, not necessarily for posterity but in order to benefit their contemporaries.

I have tried, in the translations, to convey not only the sense of the original but the rhythm as well. Very often, it is the rhythm which lends color and power to the thought. Some quotations leaped from the page straight into English, others required effort. None of them is perfect. But then, as Confucius said, "Seek perfection in no man."

Tony Blishen

Chapter I
The Essentials of Character

Morality

Do not act improperly nor look at, listen to, or speak of that which is improper.
— *Confucius: Analects*

Do not do to others that which you would not wish done to you.
— *Ibid.*

The young should respect their parents at home and obey their teachers abroad, be trustworthy and cautious in speech, love their fellow men and seek out the virtuous.
— *Ibid.*

The Master said, "comfort the old, win the trust of friends and cherish the young."
— *Ibid.*

The gentleman knows morality, the rogue merely advantage.
— *Ibid.*

To me, wealth and position acquired without virtue are merely a passing cloud.
— *Ibid.*

The man who maintains virtue in adversity will not deviate from it in success.
— *Meng Ke: Mencius*

The man of character does not lose the innocence of childhood.
— *Ibid.*

Sympathy is the beginning of humanity, shame is the beginning of righteousness, concession is the beginning of propriety, and knowledge of right and wrong is the beginning of wisdom….Like the four limbs of a body, with them, all can be accomplished; but without them not even one's parents can be supported.
— *Ibid.*

Openness brings clarity, prejudice brings obscurity, honesty brings understanding, falsehood brings hindrance, integrity brings vitality and exaggeration brings confusion. The gentleman has a care for these six which defined the difference between the great king Yu and the despot Jie.
— *Xun Kuang: Xunzi*

The gentleman is easy in acquaintance but difficult in familiarity, anxious but not afraid, fearful of disaster but prepared for sacrifice, eager for advantage but not at the cost of wrongdoing, sociable but not cloying, and eloquent but not deceptive. However universal, the gentleman is not ordinary.
— *Ibid.*

The gentleman is not unscrupulous in seeking advantage; he avoids harm with foresight and shame with caution and is courageous in principle.
— *Ibid.*

Do not feel shame in poverty but in the inability to tread the path of principle; see no sorrow in the brevity of one's own life but see it in the want of the people.
— *Liu An: Huainanzi*

There are three components of the virtuous character: first integrity, second principle, third ideals.
— *Xun Yue: The Mirror of History*

Put national causes first and personal grudges last.
— *Sima Qian: Record of History*

Seek not the advantage of a moment but give thought to the enrichment of the generations to come.
— *Ouyang Xiu: Record of the Yanhong Dyke*

Grieve before the grief of others, enjoy after the joy of others.
— *Fan Zhongyan: Record of Yueyang Tower*

The straightforward person speaks from the heart and acts justly.
— *Lü Kun: Lamentations*

Observe morality, value honor, esteem reputation.
— *Wang Fuzhi: An Interpretation of the Classic of History*

A gentleman has not the leisure to worry over attainment or the lack of it, or household hunger or common perceptions of honor and disgrace, profit

and loss or social hierarchy.
— *Zeng Guofan: Letters of Zeng Guofan to His Family*

Resolve

First comes virtue, then achievement and last the propagation of one's own views.
— *Zuo Qiuming: Chronicle of Zuo*

The difficulty with determination is not overcoming others but overcoming oneself.
— *Han Fei: Han Feizi*

The man of high ideals may despise wealth and position, righteousness may look down upon dukes and princes, and inner cultivation may disregard the outer world.
— *Xun Kuang: Xunzi*

Without a righteous cause even bravery will not suffice. — *Liu An: Huainanzi*

How can a sparrow know the aspirations of a swan?
— *Sima Qian: Record of History*

Whales do not swim in pools or swans land in puddles. For why? Because of the extent of their aspirations.
— *Liu Xiang: Garden of Stories*

The great man must have aspirations that extend to the four corners of the earth.
— *Li Bai: Letter to Pei Kuan on His Appointment to Anzhou*

To keep to the path of righteousness, to realize ideals
and not to delude oneself. These qualities are not
easily found.
— *Liu Zongyuan: The Story of the Falcon*

Resolve creates a root, just as trees grow in girth from
tiny seed to the span of two hands and from thence to
tip the clouds.
— *Cheng Hao, Cheng Yi: Collection of the Two Chengs*

Resolve should be fixed and unwavering, firm and not
loose.
— *Chen Chun*

Ambition without purpose is like a rudderless boat
or a horse without a bit, all adrift and destination
unknown.
— *Wang Shouren*

Resolve does not seek the easily accomplished, nor
should the management of affairs skirt difficulties.
— *Fan Ye: Book of Later Han*

Be resolute even in danger.
— *Book of Rites*

I must uphold my ideals through a thousand deaths
without regret.
— *Qu Yuan: Sorrow at Parting*

Steadfastness

Be steadfast in the face of crisis.
— *Confucius: Analects*

The gentleman does not seek life at the expense of virtue; rather he sacrifices life for the sake of virtue.
— *Ibid.*

I desire both virtue and life but if I cannot have both then I would trade life for virtue.
— *Meng Ke: Mencius*

Where there is no craving for wealth and position, where aspiration is unchanged by poverty and there is no submission to power, that is greatness.
— *Ibid.*

Do not seek empty fame, do not fear slander, act in the path of righteousness, improve oneself and resist the influence of material things, that is how to be a gentleman.
— *Xun Kuang: Xunzi*

Better honorable poverty than ill gotten gains, better glorious death than a life bought by shame.
— *Record of Rites Compiled by Dai De*

All come to death, some as heavily as Mount Tai, some as light as a goose feather.
— *Sima Qian: Letter to Ren An*

A gentleman does not waste his life, nor does he throw it away.
— *Chen Shou: Records of Three Kingdoms*

The great man would rather be broken jade than whole earthenware.
— *Li Baiyao: Book of Northern Qi*

Character is best manifest through tribulation.
— *Su Shi: Letter to Ouyang Xiu*

Be steadfast in the face of danger and disaster and
without temptation in the face of fame and wealth.
— *Su Shi: Letter of Thanks to Emperor Renzong*

Live life as a hero, be a heroic spirit even after death.
— *Li Qingzhao: Poem: Wu River*

If a life may be sacrificed for the nation, how then
can it be possible to evade disaster and seek fortune
merely for one's own sake?
— *Lin Zexu: Poem of Farewell to His Family*

Self Improvement

Heaven's progress is inexorable, self improvement is endless.
— *Book of Changes*

Sheer strength may overcome others, but true power
lies in self improvement.
— *Li Er: Laozi*

Do not blame heaven, do not rebuke others.
— *Confucius: Analects*

The self aware do not blame others and those that
know fate do not blame heaven. Those that blame
others will always be troubled and those that blame
heaven lack will.
— *Xun Kuang: Xunzi*

It is better to rely upon oneself than upon others.
— *Han Fei: Han Feizi*

To command others first command yourself, to
criticize others first criticize yourself, to know others

first know yourself.
— *Lü Buwei: Lü's Spring and Autumn Annals*

Man must first act before he can be commended and first strive before winning approval.
— *Yang Xiong: Words to Live By*

One should rely on one's own sense of invulnerability for protection and not on gods and demons.
— *Ge Hong: Baopuzi (The Master Who Embraces Simplicity)*

Make a habit of unremitting effort; forge a path of daily renewal.
— *Liu Yuxi: Poetry of Questions on the Wheel of Life*

Man cannot live in a state of dependence, for nothing comes of it.
— *Yuan Zhen*

Without effort even the strong may die unnoticed but with effort even the weak may achieve posterity.
— *Ouyang Xiu: Epitaph for Zhang Jun*

A man should not seek ill gotten riches nor should he labor after poverty.
— *Su Shi: Letter to Mei Yaochen*

True ambition comes from within oneself.
— *Fang Xiaoru: Collection of the Humble Studio*

Self Discipline

The gentleman makes demands of himself; the rogue makes demands of others.
— *Confucius: Analects*

Few mistakes arise from self-restraint.
— *Ibid.*

A gentleman must bear in mind these nine
considerations: clarity of sight, acuteness of hearing,
warmth of expression, modesty of bearing, sincerity
of speech, skill in affairs, enquiry in doubt, the
consequences of anger and morality in acquisition.
— *Ibid.*

A gentleman should beware of three things: in lusty
youth, lechery; in vigorous manhood, brawling; in
feeble old age, greed.
— *Ibid.*

Disaster and fortune, both are brought upon oneself.
— *Meng Ke: Mencius*

Inaction must precede action.
— *Ibid.*

Lack of self-esteem invites humiliation.
— *Ibid.*

Arrogance must be restrained, desire must be curbed,
ambition must not be sated and pleasure must be limited.
— *Book of Rites*

Avoid excess and the body will come to no harm.
— *Han Fei: Han Feizi*

Lust and anger are common to both the sage and the
stupid alike. The sage can exercise restraint and curb
them; the stupid lack restraint and lose thereby.
— *Wu Jing: Outline of Affairs during the Zhenguan
Reign of the Tang Dynasty*

Self-restraint conquers anger and reason conquers fear.
— *Cheng Hao, Cheng Yi: Collection of the Two Chengs*

Do not let selfishness harm the common good.
— *Su Zhe: Luancheng Collection*

The complete man is not self-satisfied and the self-satisfied man is not complete.
— *Luo Dajing: Dew of Jade in the Forest of Cranes*

Good comes to the restrained and evil to the self-indulgent.
— *Lü Kun: Lamentations*

However much one may try, to act as one ought not, or without regard to one's status, or against the law can reap no benefit. Even if it does, the benefit will be small.
— *Ibid.*

There is nothing so hidden that it may not be seen or so small that it may not be apparent. For this reason the gentleman is circumspect even in solitude.
— *Book of Rites*

Prudence in private life preserves integrity.
— *Li Ao*

Perseverance

Failure to persevere in small matters confuses the grand plan.
— *Confucius: Analects*

Perseverance brings success and tolerance adds virtue.
— *Classic of History*

The possession of virtue, wisdom, competence and
the ability to direct is usually due to experience of
disaster.
— *Meng Ke: Mencius*

When heaven bestows a great task it first tests the
spirit, strains the muscles, starves the stomach and
saps the body to create a determination that achieves
what was not possible before.
— *Ibid.*

Those with a sense of suffering do not fear others,
those who make demands of themselves are not easily
regulated by others, those who are scrupulous over small
things need have no fear for the large and those who are
presently sincere need not fear future humiliation.
— *Yan Zun: A Guide to Morality*

Because the short-sighted cannot accept petty
humiliation, they suffer great loss in the end.
— *Liu Shao: Records of People*

To maintain composure in anger and self-control in
joy. That is the most difficult.
— *Chen Shou: Records of Three Kingdoms*

Endurance can avert disaster.
— *Ye Mengde: Summer Thoughts*

If there is no sacrifice there is no gain, if there is no
perseverance there is no reward.
— *Su Xun: Collection of Su Xun*

The gentleman who seeks a distant goal must be prepared to wait; he who seeks great achievement must endure.
— *Su Shi: On the Western Han Philosopher Jia Yi*

Withstand insult and humiliation with forbearance, and achievement lies in the future.
— *Su Shi: On Marquess Liu*

Peace comes to those who can bear insult and survival to those who can endure humiliation.
— *Liu Xiang: Garden of Stories*

Use the word "endure" as a motto.
— *Lu You*

Do not brag of a moment's satisfaction or be downcast at a moment's disappointment.
— *Feng Menglong: Stories to Caution the World*

One should be like the sacred dragon; able to stretch, withdraw and change at will, untrammeled by man or matter. To bind oneself to others is to lose the power of decision and become like an ox or goat, driven hither and thither. So it is that the wise and knowledgeable see things clearly, do not hanker after the outward and follow the dictates of their own heart. How then can they be driven by circumstance?
— *Lü Kun: Lamentations*

Not to be disturbed by the ill opinion of others; that suffices to become a gentleman.
— *Fang Xiaoru: On Blame*

Modesty

With pride comes harm and with modesty advantage.
That is the will of heaven.
— *Classic of History*

Because you do not give yourself airs, none dispute
your ability; because you do not boast, none question
your achievements.
— *Ibid.*

Those who suffer from self-regard do not achieve
fame, egotists do not gain prominence, self-promotion
achieves nothing and the supercilious do not become
leaders.
— *Li Er: Laozi*

To take pride in wealth and position is to harm
oneself.
— *Ibid.*

The absence of self-display allows achievement to the
inconspicuous.
— *Ibid.*

What is empty may be filled, hence the saying that a
void may conquer form.
— *Ibid.*

A man may be aware of his prominence but should
still conduct himself modestly and eschew an
overbearing manner.
— *Ibid.*

To know renown but to live humbly like a mere
stream under heaven; only then is virtue enough to

return to simple truth.
— *Ibid.*

Those who treat others well do so by regarding
themselves as less than others.
— *Ibid.*

It is normal to loathe those who are full of themselves
and to like those who are modest.
— *Book of Changes*

Modesty and respect for others is a means of
maintaining one's own place.
— *Ibid.*

Modesty adds glory to those with status and
invulnerability to those without. Only gentlemen can
be always thus.
— *Ibid.*

Do not boast of one's virtue nor brag of one's
achievements.
— *Confucius: Analects*

To use one's ability to bully others is no way to win
people over; but if one's ability is displayed modestly
then there are none who cannot be won over.
— *Zhuang Zhou: Zhuangzi*

Rid oneself of self-satisfaction, live virtuously and will
there not be love wherever you go?
— *Ibid.*

Intelligence with modesty. That is virtue.
— *Xun Kuang: Xunzi*

Strength with arrogance is weakened by arrogance but weakness with arrogance is the road to destruction.
— *Guan Zhong: Guanzi*

The humble will be satisfied and the self-satisfied will be humbled.
— *Collected Sayings of Confucius*

Humility is the root of all virtue; pride is the peak of all faults.
— *Wang Shouren: Record of Teaching*

The greater the arrogance, the less the ability.
— *Shen Juyun: Sayings from Shen Juyun*

Tolerance and Generosity

Tolerance derives from knowledge of custom and justice derives from tolerance. Rule derives from justice and beyond rule there is heaven. Beyond heaven there is the way and beyond the way lies eternity and life preserved.
— *Li Er: Laozi*

Like the very earth itself, the gentleman must accept its burdens with generosity.
— *Book of Changes*

The gentleman respects the worthy and accepts the ordinary, encourages the virtuous and pities the incompetent.
— *Confucius: Analects*

To be hard on oneself but not on others puts grievance at a distance.
— *Ibid.*

Those who cannot accept others will lack intimates and those without intimates are abandoned.
— *Zhuang Zhou: Zhuangzi*

Tolerance of all and harm to none. That is the very pinnacle.
— *Ibid.*

Gentlemen measure themselves straitly but welcome others. In measuring themselves straitly they are an example to all; in welcoming others they show tolerance that allows great deeds in common.
— *Xun Kuang: Xunzi*

Tolerant virtue embraces all.
— *Collected Sayings of Confucius*

Demand not perfection of others but seek to know one's own defects.
— *Classic of History*

There is nothing that the man of true virtue cannot accept, be it insult or to live in humiliation.
— *Li Er: Laozi*

The essence of Confucius lies in loyalty and forgiveness and in nothing else.
— *Confucius: Analects*

Not to dwell upon past wrongs, that is the measure of the truly virtuous.
— *Zhu Xi: Commentary on the Four Books*

When you encounter ill will, think about yourself.
— *Mo Di: Mozi*

See the good that is and do not ask for more, accept
the present and do not look in the past.
— *Han Yu: On Dispraise*

Tolerance grows with experience.
— *Xue Xuan: Record of Reading*

Do not treat people harshly; harshness drives away the
thoughtful.
— *Hong Zicheng: Vegetable Roots Discourse*

Repay spite with honesty and virtue with virtue.
— *Confucius: Analects*

The gentleman does not think ill of others before
the fact, or instantly suspect their insincerity or take
pleasure in their shortcomings; the gentleman rejoices
in helping others achieve and looks to the future.
— *Record of Rites Compiled by Dai De*

The generous man does not vilify others for his own
profit or the virtuous man damage others for his own
glory.
— *Stratagems of the Warring States*

The gentleman does not condemn others for
their shortcomings, or force them to attempt the
impossible, or vent fury upon them for their dislikes.
— *Wang Tong: True Sayings*

Grant favor without motive but remember
obligations.
— *Zhu Bailu: Household Maxims*

Integrity

Lack of integrity breeds lack of confidence.
— *Li Er: Laozi*

Empty promises enjoy little confidence.
— *Ibid.*

I believe in the reliable and the unreliable both; that is
the way to build trust.
— *Ibid.*

The nearer the truth, the more trustworthy.
— *Confucius: Analects*

How can a gentleman earn trust without integrity?
— *Meng Ke: Mencius*

The great man may not be reliable in all that he
says or consistent in all that he does but he inhabits
morality.
— *Ibid.*

Dull integrity is better than polished cunning.
— *Han Fei: Han Feizi*

Seek honesty before ability.
— *Liu An: Huainanzi*

Integrity is at the center of all.
— *Tan Qiao: The Book of Transformations*

Change what you say and there is no trust, alter your
instructions and they will not be followed.
— *Ouyang Xiu*

Victory in battle is temporary, preserving trust is forever.
— *Feng Menglong: Romance of the Kingdoms of the Eastern Zhou Dynasty*

A man whose word cannot be trusted, whose actions are unprincipled, who seeks only advantage and for whom there is nothing that may not be overthrown, may truly be called a rogue.
— *Xun Kuang: Xunzi*

The deeds of those whose word cannot be trusted will be fruitless.
— *Mo Di: Mozi*

If there is no trust between a ruler and his ministers, the people will be derisive and society unstable; if there is no integrity amongst officials, the young will not respect the old and there will be contempt between high and low; if there is no trust in reward and punishment, the people will transgress and orders will not be carried out; if there is no trust in friendship there will be division and disagreement and no intimacy; if there is no trust in crafts, utensils will be faulty and colors adulterated.
— *Lü Buwei: Lü's Spring and Autumn Annals*

Without trust there will be no help in disaster, and destruction will be sure.
— *Zuo Qiuming: Chronicle of Zuo*

Without trust, no man can stand.
— *Ibid.*

Contentment

Stifle desire, seal its gates and lead an untroubled life.
Open the gates to desire and its pursuit and life will
be beyond help.
— *Li Er: Laozi*

There is no greater disaster than not to know
contentment, and no greater sin than greed.
— *Ibid.*

To be content avoids humiliation, to know one's
limits avoids danger. This is permanence.
— *Ibid.*

Unbridled avarice diminishes a man.
— *Wang Bi: Commentaries on Laozi*

Fortunate are the contented!
— *Li Er: Laozi*

In morality compare yourself with those superior to
you and know shame, in desire compare yourself with
those inferior to you and know contentment.
— *Xun Yue: The Mirror of Telling the History*

The contented are not seduced by power or profit.
— *Liu An: Huainanzi*

Discontent leads to unfulfilled desire.
— *Chen Shou: Records of Three Kingdoms*

The contented do not seek more than they already
have. The discontented desire all that they do not
have and thus exist in perpetual want, whereas the

contented are satisfied wherever they are.
— *Ji Kang: An Answer to Xiang Xiu on Keeping Healthy*

It is not riches or fame that are difficult to acquire. It is contentment, and freedom from fear of the lack of it.
— *Ibid.*

Excessive enjoyment induces grief, and overindulgence in desire breeds calamity.
— *Wu Jing: Outline of Affairs during the Zhenguan Reign of the Tang Dynasty*

The contented are happy in poverty and the discontented miserable in wealth.
— *Lin Bu: Record of Self-Questioning*

Abstinence

The gentleman takes joy in virtue and the rogue in desire.
— *Book of Rites*

In the building of character there is nothing better than the diminution of desire. Those whose desires are few may lose some of their virtue as may those whose desires are many. But the loss will not be great.
— *Meng Ke: Mencius*

Desire defeats judgment and indulgence conquers propriety.
— *Zuo Qiuming: Chronicle of Zuo*

Follow the path of abstinence and you will come to no harm.
— *Guan Zhong: Guanzi*

Indulge desire and your days are numbered!
— *The Spring and Autumn Annals of Minister Yan Ying*

To lose honor through insatiable greed is a step towards disaster.
— *Chen Shou: Records of Three Kingdoms*

If desires are many, so, too, are exploitable weaknesses.
— *Lü Buwei: Lü's Spring and Autumn Annals*

Happiness lies in inaction and disaster in desire.
— *Han Ying*

Curb desire and one's conduct is restrained, be tempted by material wealth and one's will is weakened.
— *Fan Ye: Book of Later Han*

Remember that fragrant fish-bait conceals a hook.
— *Li Qunyu: Releasing Fish*

Once succumb to desire, then follows the flaming snare.
— *Bai Juyi: The Crane*

Absence of desire inspires pure conduct and gross desire breeds a muddy soul.
— *Du Guangting: The Way to True Morality*

Desire may weaken strength but strength does not surrender to desire.
— *Zhu Xi: Commentary on the Four Books*

Mildness

Discerning the small is called enlightenment and strength is called mildness.
— *Li Er: Laozi*

Strength is not strength, mildness is strength.
— *Wang Bi: Commentaries on Laozi*

The sharpened blade does not keep its edge, and better to refrain than take all. Who can save a mountain of jade and gold when pride in wealth and position bequeaths only harm? To give way gracefully is the way of heaven.
— *Li Er: Laozi*

The weak attract sympathy and the strong grievance.
— *Fan Ye: Book of Later Han*

Strength may be damaged and sharpness blunted.
— *Zhuang Zhou: Zhuangzi*

Iron may break gold but water remains whole.
— *Ge Hong: Baopuzi (The Master Who Embraces Simplicity)*

What is too hard can break and what is too soft can crumble. The sages stand between soft and hard and thus can follow the way.
— *Liu An: Huainanzi*

Hard is an accumulation of soft, and strength is an accumulation of weakness. Observe this process of accumulation and you will know whether the trend is towards disaster or success.
— *Ibid.*

Harshness imposed upon others wins no friends.
— *Book of Changes*

It is not cowardice to adapt with the times or bend like a reed; it is not violence to make a determined stand. To manage change with righteousness is to know when to step forward and when to step aside.
— *Xun Kuang: Xunzi*

The sages withdraw in order to advance; one takes the crooked in order to be straight. Thus one may take a dangerous road or a desolate path to reach a glorious goal.
— *Liu An: Huainanzi*

A gentleman understands the need to withdraw the better to advance and thus suffers insult in silence; he knows the need give way humbly the better to achieve victory and thus never hesitates to bow his head. This in the end snatches fortune from disaster.
— *Liu Shao: Records of People*

Soft but strong, formless yet solid.
— *Lü Buwei: Lü's Spring and Autumn Annals*

To divine the invisible is to know the visible, to reveal the soft is to display the hard.
— *Wang Anshi*

Meditation

Tranquility is a principle of the universe.
— *Li Er: Laozi*

Haste will stumble and impetuosity will lose the initiative.
— *Ibid.*

Still muddy water and it will clear, invigorate calm and it will last.
— *Ibid.*

Tranquility creates spirituality but impetuosity loses it. Spirituality comes and goes within the heart.
— *Guan Zhong: Guanzi*

Bring calm to disorder and it will order itself.
— *Ibid.*

Remain upright and calm and virtue will increase day by day.
— *Ibid.*

Calmness enables concentration and concentration of thought enables independence.
— *Ibid.*

Without indifference to desire there can be no enlightenment, without tranquility there can be no attainment afar.
— *Liu An: Huainanzi*

Fine schemes are born of the tranquil mind and boundless vision enables their fruition.
— *Deng Xi: Deng Xizi*

Only tranquillity and deep thought bring true clarity of mind.
— *Yao Chong: Admonitions*

Those that can examine themselves in tranquility can command others.
— *Su Xun: On Regulation*

Once succumb to temptation, and there is not a moment's peace.
— *Xue Xuan: Record of Reading*

Self Criticism

Correct oneself, make no demands on others and there can be no grievance.
— *Book of Rites*

When you see virtue in others examine yourself to see if you possess it; when you see faults in others, be anxious lest you too possess them. Be glad if you find virtue and disgusted if you find vice.
— *Xun Kuang: Xunzi*

Do not forget what has gone before but use it as a guide to what is to come.
— *Stratagems of the Warring States*

To accept the views of others is called wisdom, self-examination is called sagacity and self-control is called strength.
— *Sima Qian: Record of History*

Do not regard the absence of fault as virtue itself but see the correction of fault as excellence.
— *Sima Guang: Comprehensive Mirror to Aid in Government*

Ponder the morning's faults at night and repent yesterday's mistakes today.
— *Yan Zhitui: The Family Instructions of Master Yan*

It is unworthy to get the better of others by quickness of mind, or by wider knowledge and eloquence, or by strength of decision. What is worthy of a gentleman is that he should consider his own virtue insufficient and his attempts at improvement inadequate.
— *Wang Tong: True Sayings*

Self-criticism leaves effort to spare and condemning others creates misunderstanding. If a gentleman is not self-forgiving then he will reap the benefits of self-criticism. Self-criticism is the basis of self-cultivation.
— *Hu Hong: On Knowledge*

Daily self-criticism corrects fault, its absence encourages error.
— *Zhu Xi: Commentary on the Four Books*

To the self-critical every event is a tonic for self-improvement, and every criticism of others a weapon.
— *Hong Zicheng: Vegetable Roots Discourse*

Check every ill thought, correct every impulse.
— *Xue Xuan: Record of Reading*

Every mistake adds to wisdom.
— *Feng Menglong: Stories to Caution the World*

It is only I that can destroy myself and if I do not, who else can?
— *Lü Kun: Lamentations*

To forgive oneself on the grounds that one's sins are minor and to continue in error with a light heart can only lead to even greater sin.
— *Fang Bao: On the Origins of Error*

Chapter II
The Quest for Knowledge

Giving Value to Learning

Where three are together, one must be my teacher.
— *Confucius: Analects*

If I acquire truth at dawn I will die happy at dusk.
— *Ibid*

Learning does not discriminate.
— *Ibid*

Dedicated study and wide reading bring
understanding of both past and present.
— *Ouyang Xiu*

Knowledge is power.
— *Wang Chong: Discourses Weighed in the Balance*

Enshrine learning within life and it will last a lifetime.
— *Han Yu*

Love of learning itself approaches wisdom.
— *Book of Rites*

Study and you will realize your lack of learning.
— *Ibid.*

Knowledge follows realization of ignorance.
— *Zhuang Zhou: Zhuangzi*

It is wise to know one's ignorance and foolish to
pretend to knowledge.
— *Li Er: Laozi*

Unworked jade will never make a vessel and a man
without learning will never come to understanding.
— *Book of Rites*

The studious man improves with study.
— *Stratagems of the Warring States*

All matter has both long and short, so it is with men.
Thus the studious borrow the strengths of others to
remedy their own shortcomings.
— *Lü's Spring and Autumn Annals*

Not to study and to ignore learning is to be blind to
the principle of things.
— *Book of Han*

It is better to make one's own net than to envy the
fisherman on the river bank.
— *Ibid.*

Study reduces mistakes.
— *Lü Kun: Lamentations*

Books are like medicine. Read them well and you will
cure ignorance.
— *Liu Xiang*

Only through study can man's innate genius appear in all its glory.
— *Wu Jing: Outline of Affairs during the Zhenguan Reign of the Tang Dynasty*

In time, the accumulation of learning and mastery of reason improve character so that darkness is lightened and weakness becomes strength.
— *Cheng Hao, Cheng Yi: Collection of the Two Chengs*

Study each day and learning will not be forgotten, strive in all and you will never fail.
— *Xu Gan: Balanced Discourses*

Failure to study debilitates.
— *Zhu Xi, Lü Zuqian: Reflections on Things at Hand*

Love of Learning

Love learning above all.
— *Zuo Qiuming: Chronicle of Zuo*

Study as if it were difficult to succeed and in success fear to lose learning.
— *Confucius: Analects*

Achievement in learning comes only by studying as the starving seeks food or the frozen seeks clothing.
— *Zhu Xi*

To learn is to love learning, to love learning is to seek it and to seek it is to gain it.
— *Cheng Yi*

In study, a gentleman is not merely satisfied with what he knows but regrets what he does not know.
— *Chen Liang*

To study and then to revise, is that not also a joy?
— *Confucius: Analects*

Love of learning is better than learning itself and joy in learning exceeds even that.
— *Ibid.*

If you do not admire its art there can be no joy in learning.
— *Book of Rites*

Learning resembles planting trees; you may enjoy their blossom in spring and their fruit in autumn.
— *Yan Zhitui: The Family Instructions of Master Yan*

The writing of those devoted to books is remarkable and the technique of those devoted to skill is outstanding.
— *Pu Songling: Strange Stories from a Chinese Studio*

Method

Enquire widely, choose the best and follow it, observe widely and note it.
— *Confucius: Analects*

Study widely, question closely, consider prudently, define clearly and put into practice carefully.
— *Book of Rites*

Better no books at all than blind belief in them.
— *Meng Ke: Mencius*

Those that know do not display it and those that display it do not know.
— *Li Er: Laozi*

There can be no enlightenment without the will to learn and no success without the will to work.
— *Xun Kuang: Xunzi*

Those who study without companions become ignorant and ill informed.
— *Book of Rites*

A student should not fear that he lacks talent but that he lacks aspiration.
— *Xu Gan: Balanced Discourses*

If the stream runs clear it is because it comes from the source.
— *Zhu Xi*

To succeed in study come to it fresh each day.
— *Chao Yuezhi*

Only superior ambition and first class learning will achieve first class results.
— *Shen Deqian*

A scholar should be neither humble nor arrogant. Humility is useless—and so is arrogance.
— *Gu Yanwu: Record of Daily Study*

Study is a bow and talent its arrow. Draw the bow with skill and the arrow will strike its target.
— *Yuan Mei*

Stones from other hills will work jade.
— *Classic of Poetry*

In study there is only one way: single-minded dedication and painstaking hard work.
— *Zhu Xi*

Skill in study is to attack and to sweep. Attacking is to get to the nub of things and sweeping is to rid oneself of the irrelevant.
— *Zheng Xie*

Erudition

In breadth there is detail and in relaxation there is tension.
— *Sayings of Zhu Xi*

To study well do not seek every last detail.
— *Tao Qian*

Study widely with purpose, examine closely and think deeply.
— *Confucius: Analects*

Study widely and expound in detail but then return to simplicity.
— *Meng Ke: Mencius*

Enquire of many and retain the essence, observe widely and retain the outstanding.
— *Yang Xiong: Words to Live By*

In study value that which is important, in the important value breadth, through breadth understands the principle so that all flows as one.
— *Yan Yanzhi*

In learning, observe the many but acquire the few,
store deeply but distribute sparingly.
— *Su Shi: Random Sayings*

Study widely but refine later, let broad experience
bring essential knowledge.
— *Wang Tingxiang: Words of Caution*

In the past study was like vainly hauling a boat, now
it sails free in mid-stream.
— *Zhu Xi: The Delight of Reading* (a poem)

Essence of Thought

Plumb the mystery of words and search the hidden;
discover their inner meaning.
— *Book of Changes*

Study without thought achieves nothing and thought
without study is dangerous.
— *Confucius: Analects*

Thought is the prince of the mind. With thought
there is achievement, without it there is nothing.
— *Meng Ke: Mencius*

Perceive what lies within a word and you can infer
what is without.
— *Liu Zhiji: Comments on Works of History*

If you do not think there will be unreason, if you do
not seek you will not find, and if you do not ask you
will not know.
— *Chao Yuezhi*

Thinking is like drilling a well. First there is muddy water and then gradually it clears. Thus the thoughts of men are muddy to begin with but become clear in time.
— *Cheng Hao, ChengYi: Collection of the Two Chengs*

To study one must know how to begin and how to finish; to start one must know how to begin and to end one must know how to finish.
— *Chen Shan*

At first one must read with ardor so that the words seem to come from one's own mouth. Then one must ponder so that the meaning appears as if from one's own mind. Then you can reap the benefit.
— *Zhu Xi*

In study first spend time on that which is easy to understand; give it thought and the difficulties will melt away.
— *Lu Jiuyuan*

Read between the lines.
— *Lu Shanji*

Understanding derives from thought; if there is no thought there can be no understanding. Thought is rooted in study and if there is no study there can be no true thought. The purpose of study is to achieve understanding and understanding brings enlightenment.
— *Lu Shiyi*

Study is no obstacle to thought and the wider the study the deeper the thought; thought contributes

to study and through consideration of its difficulties
study itself acquires diligence.
— *Wang Fuzhi*

The ear must listen before it can distinguish sound,
the eye must distinguish color before it can see, the
mind must think and then perceive, without thought
there is nothing.
— *Ibid.*

Skepticism

Assemble knowledge through study, distinguish truth
through enquiry.
— *Book of Changes*

An energetic love of study bears no shame in asking
questions.
— *Confucius: Analects*

A love of enquiry enriches but restriction to oneself
breeds a narrow mind.
— *Classic of History*

For the capable to seek instruction from the
incapable, for the knowledgeable to seek information
from the ignorant, is to make the full empty and
nothing out of something.
— *Confucius: Analects*

If there is neither enquiry nor discrimination
in learning there can be neither discovery nor
clarification.
— *Sima Guang*

To be skeptical where there is no doubt, that is progress.
— *Zhang Zai*

In study, first master the art of skepticism.
— *Zhu Xi, Lü Zuqian: Reflections on Things at Hand*

Enlightenment is the conquering of doubt.
— *Li Zhi: Books to Be Burnt*

Doubt the less, comprehend the less, doubt the more comprehend the more, doubt not at all and comprehend nothing.
— *Huang Zongxi*

Enlightenment derives from skepticism and joy from painstaking enquiry.
— *Shen Juyun*

From great skepticism grows great enlightenment.
— *Recorded Sayings of Dahui Zonggao*

Scholarship comprises learning and enquiry. People today learn but do not enquire. They may read books by the thousand but it is mere stupidity.
— *Zheng Xie*

A gentleman is reserved about what he does not know.
— *Confucius: Analects*

Doubt the new and doubt the old; doubt danger and doubt peace.
— *Fang Yizhi*

The skilled skeptic does not doubt where others doubt but doubts where they do not.
— *Ibid.*

Practice

A scholar may be a man of learning but he also acts
according to moral principle.
— *Mo Di: Mozi*

The difficulty lies not in understanding but in
carrying it into practice.
— *Classic of History*

It is better to enquire than not, better to see than to
enquire, better to know than to see and better to act
than to know.
— *Xun Kuang: Xunzi*

Scholars fathom the principle of things, and those
that act seize their difficulties.
— *Ibid.*

One gains but a shallow impression from the written
word. To know absolutely you must experience it
yourself.
— *Lu You*

To know but not to act is to know but little.
— *Cheng Yi*

Knowledge and action depend upon each other just as
eyes need legs to walk and legs cannot walk without
eyes. As between first and last knowledge is first, and
as between light and heavy action is heavy.
— *Sayings of Zhu Xi*

To have just come to knowledge but not yet to have
acted, then that knowledge is still shallow. But to
have experienced it oneself is to understand fully and

beyond the knowledge of the past.
— *Zhu Xi*

True knowledge inspires action; if not, it cannot be called knowledge.
— *Wang Yangming*

The true proof of knowledge lies in action and the distilled essence of action lies in knowledge.
— *Ibid.*

Action may pluck the fruit of knowledge but knowledge knows not the fruit of action.
— *Wang Fuzhi*

Learning, enquiry, thought, discrimination and action. Of these five, action may not be abandoned.
— *Ibid.*

Innovation

To acquire all the skills of the great calligraphers in all respects without deviation is to be a slave to the brush. But to go beyond this into a realm of wonder where there are no footsteps to follow, that is mystery indeed.
— *Shen Kuo: Dream Pool Essays*

The chess master does not relinquish the records of past games but nor does he stick to them. Eminent doctors are not constrained by ancient practice but nor do they abandon it.
— *Ji Yun: Yuewei Thatched Cottage Notes*

The gentleman seeks profound learning through truth
and his own efforts and to his own benefit. His own
effort will bring mastery. If he has mastery of it he will
accumulate deep knowledge, and if he accumulates
deep knowledge he may use it on every hand. Thus it is
that gentlemen seek to profit by their own efforts.
— *Meng Ke: Mencius*

In learning there is nothing more valuable than study
through one's own effort and not from elsewhere,
hence the phrase.
— *Cheng Hao, Cheng Yi: Collection of the Two Chengs*

Learning acquired through one's own efforts is
not easily put aside, and the beliefs of those with
confidence in self are immoveable.
— *Ibid.*

Nothing excels more than one's own efforts; to have a
mind of one's own can transform all.
— *Fang Xiaoru*

To gain by oneself, to bring to fruition by oneself,
to experience for oneself and not to rely upon one's
fellows or book learning.
— *Lu Jiuyuan*

If a mind of hard won self-scholarship considers
something to be in error, then though Confucius
himself may have said it, it cannot be considered fact.
— *Wang Yangming*

The value of learning lies in self-awareness. Clinging
to the old forms has no merit.
— *Zhang Zai*

Throw out the perceptions of the past, bring on fresh ideas.
— *Zhu Xi*

Following the contrivances of others will only leave you behind. Only by striking out on your own can you be true to self.
— *Huang Tingjian*

Though you may learn the language of a myriad birds, in the end you will lack a voice of your own.
— *Zhang Shunmin*

Accumulating Knowledge

Learning is forever.
— *Xun Kuang: Xunzi*

Seek and then obtain, act and then succeed, accumulate and then achieve and act in perfection to be a sage. For sages are the ultimate states of ordinary mortals.
— *Ibid.*

Without an accumulation of small steps you cannot reach 1,000 *li*, without an accumulation of small streams there can be neither rivers nor sea.
— *Ibid.*

Trees of great girth spring from a single seed, a terrace of nine levels stands upon accumulated earth and a journey of 1,000 *li* starts with a single step.
— *Li Er: Laozi*

Accumulate learning as collecting jewels and ponder reason to enhance talent.
— *Liu Xie: The Literary Mind and the Carving of Dragons*

Practise a thousand tunes to know music, test a thousand blades to know swords.
— *Ibid.*

Mastery of a subject cannot be achieved without reading volumes; without reading generations of texts you cannot master the logic of change.
— *Huangfu Shi*

Study volumes and your pen will take wings.
— *Han Yu*

The art of study lies in ordered, gradual progress and thoughtful revision to reach the essence.
— *Zhu Xi*

Read a library of books and you will begin to understand mystery.
— *Su Shi*

Unremitting Study

Study and yet not learn but do not give up, enquire and yet not know but do not give up.
— *Book of Rites*

Increase ability day by day, add wisdom year by year and progress will resemble a river in full flood.
— *Liu Zongyuan*

The Master said: "At fifteen I had the will to learn, at thirty I stood upon my own feet, at forty nothing disconcerted me, at fifty I knew the will of heaven, at sixty I was acute in judgment and at seventy whatever I desired was within bounds."
— *Confucius: Analects*

Seek and only then acquire, act and only then achieve, accumulate and only then increase, excel and only then become a sage.
— *Xun Kuang: Xunzi*

Truly accumulate learning by lengthy study and the gates will open. Study until the end of life.
— *Ibid.*

Carve a bit and rotten wood will not break, work without rest and stone and metal can be carved.
— *Ibid.*

What others can do at once, strive to do a hundred times, what they can do in ten attempts, strive to do a thousand times. In this way the ignorant become clever and the weak strong.
— *Book of Rites*

Unremitting study exercises the soul.
— *Shi Jiao: Shizi*

In seeking the truth there is early and there is late, in implementing the truth there is favorable and unfavorable but unceasing effort will bring attainment to both.
— *Zhu Xi: Commentary on the Four Books*

A gentleman should be diligent in study unto death and fear only that his learning is incomplete.
— *Ibid.*

With unceasing study much may be harvested from little seed but ceasing study mid-way sacrifices all that has been achieved.
— *Ibid.*

The study of both archery and incantations is not the matter of a mere moment.
— *Compendium of Five Lamps*

The appearance of laziness is the beginning of despair.
— *Zhu Xi, Lü Zuqian: Reflections on Things at Hand*

Scholarship requires orderly, gradual and unceasing toil; a day's progress may seem insufficient but is more than enough if reckoned in years.
— *Zhu Shunshui*

True achievement requires a lifetime's toil.
— *Lu Shiyi*

Recognizing Error

The fault of some in study is too much. Or too little, or too lightly, or just giving up.
— *Book of Rites*

In the past they studied for themselves, but now they study to look good in the eyes of others.
— *Confucius: Analects*

If the mind is not concentrated knowledge cannot be acquired. If thought is not ordered learning can have no precision and hesitation breeds doubt.
— *Xun Kuang: Xunzi*

The gentleman does not acquire knowledge free of the advice of colleagues or without system, or merely for the sake of quantity.
— *Ibid.*

Sheep may be lost along different paths; years may be wasted in diffuse study.
— *Lie Yukou: Liezi*

Limited learning causes great confusion, and pretence to learning great folly.
— *Liu An: Huainanzi*

Those who claim that they have not the time for study would not study even if they had.
— *Ibid.*

Those who study without breadth cannot master the essentials; those who lack will cannot put them into practice
— *Yang Shi: Essence of the Two Chengs*

In study there are four defects: to acquire too much through inability to select, to acquire too little through over-concentration, to be superficial through failure to enquire and to give up through fear of difficulty.
— *Zhang Zai: Correcting Youthful Ignorance*

In the end, desire for quantity prevents fruition and where lies the use of so much if it is not of the essence?
— *Su Shi*

In study and in affairs avoid the desire for easy victory or quick results. To seek them is to circumscribe oneself and prevents attainment of the origins of things.
— *Huang Zongxi*

The great defect of learning is a thirst for fame.
— *Wang Yangming*

Scholars have two faults: broad generalization on insufficient evidence and preaching on the basis of an insufficiently formed moral character.
— *Cui Xian*

There is no greater fault in scholarship than to adhere rigidly to a view and not to modify it.
— *Gu Yanwu: Record of Daily Study*

In scholarship there are introverted scholars who regard broad learning as a ride on a runaway horse and expansive scholars who regard self reflection as narrow and limited; they are both biased, this is the great malady of scholarship.
— *Sayings of Zhu Xi*

To regard wide reading alone as scholarship is the first mistake in perception, where then is the time for consideration of enquiry, for discrimination, for thought and for action?
— *Yan Yuan: A Record of Scholarship Deposited*

Teaching and Learning

Learn then realize that one's knowledge is insufficient, teach and then realize where difficulties lie. You can

remedy the insufficiencies through reflection and conquer the difficulties through self strength, hence the saying "learning and teaching grow together."
— *Book of Rites*

Pupils may not be less than their teachers and teachers may not be brighter than their pupils. Instruction has its own order and teaching its own ways, that is all.
— *Han Yu: On Teaching*

Both principle and method may be taught, what cannot be taught are the processes of the heart and the creations of the mind.
— *Zhang Xuecheng: General Interpretation of Historiography*

In learning there is no great and small but only respect for the able.
— *Li Ruzhen: Flowers in the Mirror*

A gentleman teaches by guiding not dragging, by strength but not force and by showing the way rather than by proceeding directly.
— *Book of Rites*

Skilled singers teach their sound, skilled teachers imbue their spirit.
— *Ibid.*

Encourage the sluggard and enlighten the ignorant.
— *Ouyang Xiu*

Teaching is best when adapted to the pupil.
— *Li Zhi: Books to Be Burnt*

The teaching of the ancients preserved the old virtues, cultivated them and expanded them.
— *Lu Jiuyuan*

To nuture and to teach is difficult in the extreme but the talents of those taught must be developed to the utmost lest their lives be wasted.
— *Zhang Zai: Quotations*

Teach so as not to need to teach, that is the goal of teaching.
— *Yan Zun*

The enlightened teacher brings his pupils to take joy in learning, to be at ease and yet serious.
— *Lü Buwei: Lü's Spring and Autumn Annals*

To forbid before the act is called prevention, to study when appropriate is called timely, to teach within the pupil's ability is called orderly and mutual improvement is called emulation. These four are the wellsprings of teaching.
— *Book of Rites*

Teaching is the nurture of virtue and the curing of fault.
— *Ibid.*

Chapter III
Personal Relations

Knowledge of People

The man of simplicity does not advertise it.
— *Li Er: Laozi*

If all condemn them examine the reason, if all
applaud them, examine the reason also.
— *Confucius: Analects*

When first I knew people, I listened and believed
their conduct. Now I listen and examine their
conduct.
— *Ibid.*

Those who put store by the outward place little store
by the inward.
— *Lie Yukou: Liezi*

It is better to examine the heart than observe
appearance and better to examine action than
examine the heart.
— *Xun Kuang: Xunzi*

Observe their associates and you will learn of their
virtue or not.
— *Guan Zhong: Guanzi*

Those who fish for compliments lack both virtue and
talent.
— *Ibid.*

The arrogant lack gentility.
— *Ibid.*

Those who share ambitions compete; those who share
suffering are partners.
— *Stratagems of the Warring States*

To know others, observe the mighty to see whom
they raise up, observe the rich to see what they
bestow, observe the unfortunate to see what they will
refuse, observe the humble to see what they will not
do and observe the poor to see what they will not
take.
— *Liu An: Huainanzi*

To place importance on outward appearances but not
upon speech and behavior is futile.
— *Xun Yue: The Mirror of Telling the History*

Place little faith in those who promise much lightly.
— *Liu Shao: Records of People*

Position does not indicate worth nor stupidity the
lack of it.
— *Bai Juyi: The Pine at the Stream's Foot*

Observe what interests him and you will know the man.
— *Ouyang Xiu: Record of the Hall of Beauty*

The false hearted speak falsely and may appear honest though their heart is not. They may gain admiration for a while but in time their falsity will appear and they will be shunned.
— *Yuan Cai: Yuan's Hereditary Rules*

A moment's praise does not make a man a gentleman nor does a moment's slander make him a rogue.
— *Feng Menglong: Stories to Caution the World*

Behavior towards Others

In friendship he gave me peaches and I returned him plums.
— *Classic of Poetry*

A gentleman is open with all but partial to none, but a rogue is partial and open with none.
— *Li Er: Laozi*

A gentleman likes others on a basis of virtue, the shallow minded like others out of appeasement.
— *Book of Rites*

Those who are indifferent to others will be without intimates and those without intimates will be forever strangers.
— *Zhuang Zhou: Zhuangzi*

Those who love others will always be loved and those who respect others will always be respected.
— *Meng Ke: Mencius*

Those who give love will receive it. Bestow happiness
and it will return itself.
— *Jia Yi: New Essays*

The solid stick with the solid like glue but the empty
with the empty like ice in the midday sun.
— *Han Ying*

If there is substance to relations then there is closeness
however distant, but if there is emptiness then there is
distance however close.
— *Ibid.*

Those who bestow best do so without thought of
return but those who receive should repay favors.
— *Liu Xiang: Garden of Stories*

Treat those above without flattery and those below
without condescension.
— *Book of Changes*

When those below respect those above, it is called
respect for rank. When those above respect those below,
it is called respect for worth. They are both the same.
— *Meng Ke: Mencius*

In dealings with people emphasize the good and
ignore shortcomings and they will endure.
— *The School Sayings of Confucius*

Those who doubt others will themselves be doubted,
those who are cautious of others will meet caution in
return.
— *Tan Qiao: The Book of Transformations*

Those who oppress will be suppressed and those who are considerate will meet with consideration.
— *Ibid.*

Praise and you will be praised, slander and you will be slandered.
— *Ibid.*

Take joy in bestowing praise but do not flatter.
— *Su Xun: A First Letter to Palace Writer Ouyang*

Friendship between gentlemen is based upon shared interests, that between rogues upon common advantage.
— *Ouyang Xiu: On Cliques*

If throughout life you value mutual understanding, why needs think of gold or treasure!
— *Li Bai: Three Poems for a Friend*

Making Friends

As voice responds to voice and breath to breath, so will like seek like.
— *Book of Changes*

If a gentleman acts with probity and treats others with respect, all become brothers. How can he then suffer the lack of them?
— *Confucius: Analects*

Heads grown white together may be strangers but a chance acquaintance an old friend.
— *Sima Qian: Record of History*

Old acquaintance at first sight and understanding at first word.
— *Wang Wei: On Saying Farewell to Quan Er*

In youth rejoice at new acquaintance, in age think of old friends.
— *Han Yu*

In the past, there was nothing achieved that did not require friends.
— *Wang Anshi: Letter to Sun Shenlao*

There is no greater joy than that of fresh acquaintance.
— *Lu You: Dong Jin*

Spend time in the company of the virtuous and talented and you will not transgress.
— *Zhuang Zhou: Zhuangzi*

As a gentleman needs choose to reside in the country so should you choose friends wisely, to avoid evil and keep close to righteousness.
— *Xun Kuang: Xunzi*

Keep no company with louts.
— *Guan Zhong: Guanzi*

Those who cannot distinguish between right and wrong are not fit company.
— *Mo Di: Mozi*

Gentlemen choose first and relate later, rogues relate first and choose later. So it is that gentlemen are spared trouble but rogues are always in it.
— *Xu Gan: Balanced Discourses*

Keep no company with those whose position is high but whose morals are low. Do not become close to those whose repute and substance are doubtful.
— *Ge Hong: Baopuzi (The Master Who Embraces Simplicity)*

Avoid careless associations and choose associates as you would a teacher.
— *Jia Dao: Farewell to Scholar Shen on Returning to the East after Failing an Exam*

The company of the talented sharpens perception, that of the stupid blunts it.
— *Pi Rixiu: The Writings of Pi*

If you want to be good, you must make good friends.
— *Lü Desheng: Words for Children*

Intelligence goes with intelligence and good fellows go together.
— *Shi Nai'an: The Water Margin*

A man who is not upright and well informed will never have friends who are.
— *Shen Juyun: Sayings from Shen Juyun*

Friends come together in morality.
— *Zhu Xi: Commentary on the Four Books*

Where there is affinity in righteousness, then mutual understanding is to be valued.
— *Liu Zongyuan*

The world is full of those who know each other, but how many truly understand each other!
— *Feng Menglong: Stories to Caution the World*

In joy there are friends a plenty, in sorrow there are few.
— *Pu Songling*

There are three kinds of good friends and three kinds of bad. The good are the upright, the sincere and the well informed. The bad are those who flatter, those who slander and those who exaggerate.
— *Confucius: Analects*

Managing Friendship

To greet a friend from afar, is that not a joy?
— *Confucius: Analects*

It is rare to find a friend when in difficulty.
— *Liu E: The Travels of Lao Can*

Make no friends less than oneself.
— *Confucius: Analects*

With friends be reliable in your speech.
— *Ibid.*

Friends both encourage and learn from each other.
— *Ibid.*

A friendship of righteousness needs not constant care.
— *Guo Xiashu*

With friends throughout the world, even the edge of the universe will seem close.
— *Wang Bo: On Bidding Farewell to District Guardian Du on His Appointment to Sichuan*

The path of friendship is mutual instruction.
— *Zuo Qiuming: Chronicle of Zuo*

The congeniality of friendship fosters mutual correction.
— *Zhou Xingsi: Thousand Character Classic*

Speak of virtue when you hear it, display virtue when you see it.
— *Book of Rites*

Laughter unlocks the heart.
— *Zhuang Zhou: Zhuangzi*

Friendship is neither age nor position nor family. True friendship is of the virtue of friends.
— *Meng Ke: Mencius*

There are four principles to friendship and wealth is not among them: if a friend is close by his conduct may be corrected and if distant appreciated, in joy friendship may be enjoyed and in disaster pursued unto death.
— *Ban Gu: Discourses in the White Tiger Hall*

In friendship do not seek advantage nor avoid harm. Be not importunate nor yet trivial. Only the virtuous may achieve this.
— *Wang Tong: True Sayings*

Neither success nor failure, rise or fall, should affect feeling for old friends.
— *Wei Yingwu*

To help each other out of a constant heart, that is friendship between gentlemen.
— *Ouyang Xiu: On Cliques*

In friendship a gentleman is distant from praise but
close to correction.
— *Cui Dunli*

First thin then thick, first distant then close, first far
then near, that is the way of friendship.
— *Wang Da*

A revered friend is better than a strict teacher.
— *Shen Hanguang: Sentences from a Garden of Thorns*

Living with virtue is like dwelling with a lily; with
time you become one with its fragrance. Living
with evil is like visiting a fish market; with time you
become one with its stink.
— *Liu Xiang: Garden of Stories*

Blue dye will dye blue and yellow dye will dye yellow.
— *Mo Di: Mozi*

Those that come together through power fall apart
when it is exhausted.
— *Sima Qian: Record of History*

Seek no friendship with those of different aspirations
despite their wealth, let not poverty alter affection.
— *Fan Ye: Book of Later Han*

Those that come together to seek advantage abandon
each other in disaster; those that are joined by nature
support each other in disaster.
— *Zhuang Zhou: Zhuangzi*

Friendship with riches fails when wealth is exhausted;
friendship with beauty fails when glamour fades.
— *Stratagems of the Warring States*

Words and Deeds

Those that know do not talk and those that talk do
not know.
— *Li Er: Laozi*

The accomplished are few in words and the impatient
talk too much.
— *Book of Changes*

Zi Gong asked about gentility. The Master replied
"Act first and speak later."
— *Confucius: Analects*

The gentleman is cautious in speech but swift in deed.
— *Ibid.*

Speak without error, act without regret.
— *Ibid.*

Speak frankly and act without bias.
— *The Spring and Autumn Annals of Minister Yan Ying*

The gentleman is reserved in speech but the rogue gushes.
— *Book of Rites*

The gentleman does not mention that which can be
described but not done and does not do that which is
unmentionable.
— *Ibid.*

To speak grandly but not to deliver is to call disaster
upon oneself.
— *Ibid.*

To do what one can say, that is a treasure indeed.
— *Xun Kuang: Xunzi*

It is wise to speak when appropriate and wise, too, to be silent when appropriate.
— *Ibid.*

To speak near but mean far is the speech of excellence, to be reserved in manner but broad in application is the way of excellence.
— *Meng Ke: Mencius*

Careless speech is an injury to oneself.
— *Guan Zhong: Guanzi*

A gentleman ends friendship without rancor.
— *Stratagems of the Warring States*

Fine words damage confidence.
— *The School Sayings of Confucius*

Words should not exceed their meaning, nor actions outstrip their means.
— *Liu An: Huainanzi*

Those that can speak well of the past must apply it to the present; those that can speak well of heaven must apply it to earth.
— *Lu Jia: New Words*

Speak without regard for the consequences and it is too late for silence when disaster strikes.
— *Huan Kuan: Debates on Salt and Iron*

Speak not of the shortcomings of others nor of one's own strengths.
— *Cui Yuan: Maxims*

Knowledge is knowledge and ignorance is ignorance, this is the crux of speech: ability is ability and

inability is inability, this is the principle of action.
— *Han Ying*

Those who hold power must be cautious in its exercise, those who give orders must be cautious in their speech, thus may error and defeat be avoided.
— *Jia Yi: New Essays*

Say what you do and do what you say.
— *Sima Qian: Classic of History*

The loyal speak with sincerity and the loving with profundity.
— *Chen Shou: Records of Three Kingdoms*

Sickness enters through the mouth but disaster leaves from it.
— *Fu Xuan*

Profound speech in a shallow acquaintanceship is stupid.
— *Fan Ye: Book of Later Han*

There can be no farsighted planning with the wordy, nor permanence with the restless.
— *Wang Tong: True Sayings*

Dare to say what others will not.
— *Ouyang Xiu*

Be concise.
— *Su Shi*

The speech of those unskilled in affairs is muddled but the speech of those skilled in logic is clear.
— *Yang Wanli*

Words spoken in mutual joy lack reliability; words
spoken in hatred lack decorum.
— *Qian Qi*

Seven or eight parts action but only two or three parts
speech.
— *Xue Xuan: Record of Reading*

Words have no greater evil than a false accusation.
— *Lü Kun: Lamentations*

All speech depends upon reality alone.
— *Xue Xuan: Record of Reading*

The heart may understand what is beyond speech and
the mind may perceive what is beyond expression.
— *Cao Xueqin: The Dream of the Red Chamber*

Notes on Sources

Analects: See *Confucius*.

Bai Juyi (772 – 846): Realist poet of the Tang dynasty and one of China's greatest poets. An outstanding candidate in the imperial examinations, he became an official and later a Hanlin Academician. Bai Juyi wrote his treatise *The Forest of Stratagems* (*Ce Lin*) in 806, early in his career as an official. At the age of 44, following the production of a volume of satirical poems, he was demoted and exiled from court on the grounds that his outspoken comments on the assassination of the prime minister had usurped the functions of the official hierarchy. He was later reinstated but finally sought a provincial post where he earned a reputation as a sympathetic and effective administrator, particularly in the field of irrigation.

Ban Biao (3 – 54): Historian of the Eastern Han dynasty and father of the historian Ban Gu (q.v.). Given an official post by the Han emperor Guangwu on the recommendation of General Dou Rong whose adviser he had been, but later resigned due to ill health. Ban Biao started the *Book of Han*, which was completed by his son Ban Gu and daughter Ban Zhao.

Ban Gu (32 – 92): Historian and poet. His *Book of Han* (*Han Shu*) was the first to rearrange existing material chronologically by dynasty. It covered a period of 230 years and set a pattern which later histories followed.

Bao Zheng (999 – 1062): Scholar, author and much-praised official who served during the reign of Emperor Renzong of the Northern Song dynasty. He refused office in order to look after his elderly parents. He returned to the capital after the death of his parents and was appointed imperial censor and later Prefect of Kaifeng, a politically sensitive post where he added to his reputation for incorruptibility. He has a reputation as a symbol of justice even today.

Book of Changes (**_Zhou Yi_**): An extremely early manual for divination by the use of the Eight Trigrams (*Ba Gua*).

Book of Later Han: See *Fan Ye*.

Cao Xueqin (c.1715 – c.1764): Novelist and author of the colloquial novel *Dream of the Red Chamber* (*Hong Lou Meng*), a work which was ten years in the writing and which realistically describes life in a wealthy but increasingly corrupt and licentious Chinese household. It has been translated many times. Perhaps the best English translation is that of David Hawkes (and later John Minford) under the novel's alternative title the *Story of the Stone* (*Shi Tou Ji*).

Cao Zhi (192 – 232): Younger brother of Cao Pi who became ruler and then king of the state of Wei despite their father Cao Cao's initial preference for Cao Zhi. His later poetry reflects the grief and resentment that he felt at his situation. He is also credited with being the originator of Buddhist chant in China.

Chao Yuezhi (1059 – 1129): Scholar and official.

Chen Chun (1159 – 1217): Philosopher of the Southern Song dynasty. In his later years a disciple of Zhu Xi (q.v.).

Chen Liang (1143 – 1194): A disputatious philosopher and poet of the Southern Song dynasty. He advocated a form of realism in government. Imprisoned twice on the basis of false allegations, he died before he could take up the official post to which he had been appointed.

Chen Shan: Song dynasty scholar of the mid 12th century.

Chen Shou (233 – 297): Historian and military official who started writing his history of the kingdoms of Wei, Shu and Wu, the *Record of Three Kingdoms* (*San Guo Zhi*), in 280. It recorded events of the previous 60 years. Subsequent historians have regarded it with respect but as not without personal bias.

Chen Zi'ang (659 – 700): Able official who wrote knowledgeably of the political and military problems of the western border regions, a political reformer and (conservative) poet who fell out of favor, resigned and died in rural isolation at the age of 41. Regarded as a better poet than politician.

Cheng Hao (1032 – 1085): Educator and philosopher whose teachings, with those of his close associate Cheng Yi (1033 – 1107) formed the Rationalist school of Neo-Confucianism.

Cheng Yi (1033 – 1107): See *Cheng Hao*.

***Classic of Poetry* (*Shi Jing*)**: Also known as *The Book of Songs*. The earliest collection of Chinese poetry and song, dating from the 11th to 6th centuries BC. It comprised court odes, folk songs and chants for sacrificial ceremonies together with other material, 305 items in all.

***Compendium of Five Lamps* (*Wu Deng Hui Yuan*)** (1252): Compiled by the monk Pu Ji of the Song dynasty. A Zen text ascribed to the Lingyin Temple near Hangzhou.

***Confucius* (*Kongzi*)** (551 – 479 BC): Philosopher and founder of one of the principal schools of Chinese philosophy. Often mentioned in the same breath with his disciple Mencius. The *Analects* (*Lun Yu*), also known as the *Analects of Confucius*, is regarded as a record of the sayings and opinions of Confucius and his disciples, as well as of the discussions they held. Written during the 5th to 3rd centuries BC, it is the fundamental work of Confucianism and continues to exert a strong influence on Chinese and East Asian thought and values.

Cui Dunli: Scholar and writer of the Southern Song dynasty (1127 – 1279).

Cui Xian (1478 – 1541): Ming scholar appointed to the Hanlin Academy who, despite his abilities, was demoted or posted to the provinces several times during his career either because of the power of the court eunuchs or because he fell out of favor with the emperor.

Cui Yuan (77 – 142): Scholar, official and calligrapher noted for his running script.

Dai Zhen (1724 – 1777): Qing dynasty official and literary figure of wide scientific interests who criticized Neo-Confucianism and regarded the individual as paramount. He is considered one of the pioneers of scientific study in China.

Debates on Salt and Iron (***Yan Tie Lun***): See *Huan Kuan*.

Deng Xi (545 – 501 BC): Thinker and reformer who believed that the rule of rite should be replaced by the rule of law and produced his own manual of punishments. *Deng Xizi* is considered to be a record of his sayings and opinions.

Dong Zhongshu (179 – 104 BC): Western Han dynasty philosopher and scholar who expanded the principles of Confucianism into a theory of government.

Du Fu (712 – 770): Tang realist poet who also followed an official career. One of China's best known and greatest poets.

Du Guangting (850 – 933): Daoist scholar, philosopher, poet, calligrapher and novelist who pursued an official career but spent his later years in hermetic contemplation at Mount Qingchengshan one of the original centers of Daoism. He wrote one of the earliest martial arts short stories and two poems where the number of characters in each line increased by two every line from the original two to 28 and 30.

Fan Jun (1102 – 1150): Scholar, official and philosopher.

Fan Ye (398 – 445): Historian and imperial official. He fell victim to intrigue, did not complete his history, the *Book of Later Han* (*Hou Han Shu*) and was executed together with many of his family.

Fan Zhongyan (989 – 1052): Northern Song official and soldier who was several times the victim of intrigue because of his outspoken views. Recalled to service in 1040 after the establishment of the Xixia dynasty on the North West frontier, he was dispatched to the border and found the Song frontier garrisons, after 30 years of peace, defective in organization, logistics and strategy and incapable of winning the border war. Following Xixia successes, he stabilized the border with fortifications and garrisons (notably Dashuncheng) and a policy of generosity towards border tribes.

Fang Bao (1668 – 1749): Qing official and essayist who was implicated in the publication (he wrote the preface) of a book regarded as inflammatory, whose author, Dai Mingshi, was impeached. Fang Bao was condemned to death and spent several years in prison but continued to write. He was eventually released after the death of the Emperor Kangxi and pardoned. Several hundred people were caught up in the case which achieved some notoriety.

Fang Xiaoru (1357 – 1402): Well known Ming scholar.

Fang Yizhi (1611 – 1671): Philosopher and scientist who became a Buddhist monk after the fall of the Ming dynasty in 1644 and organized an underground movement aimed at the restoration of the dynasty.

Feng Menglong (1574 – 1646): Novelist and dramatist. *Stories to Caution the World* (*Jing Shi Tong Yan*) is a reworking of existing material. He reworked two other books *Illustrious Words to Instruct the World* (*Yu Shi Ming Yan*) and *Stories to Awaken the World* (*Xing Shi Heng Yan*).

Fu Xuan (217 – 278): Scholar, official and poet. In 268, he advanced five proposals for improving agriculture and the life of the peasants in order to cope with the floods and famine of the time.

Ge Hong (c.281 – 341): Daoist scholar and theorist and famed seeker of the elixir of life or pill of immortality. After appointments as an official he became a hermit on Mount Luofu in the northern part of Guangdong province.

Gu Yanwu (1613 – 1682): A Neo-Confucian polymath who contributed to many fields of learning. He played a part in resistance to the invaders as the Ming dynasty collapsed and is regarded as one of the pioneers of learning during the Qing dynasty.

Guan Yin Zi: A Daoist work, said to have been written by Guan Yin at the the end of the Spring and Autumn period.

Guan Zhong (? – 645 BC): Also known as Guanzi. Statesman of the early Spring and Autumn period.

Guo Xiashu: Poet of the period of the Three Kingdoms who dedicated five poems to the philosopher and musician Ji Kang (q.v.).

Guo Zuo (c.448 – 515): Scholar and official under the Northern Wei dynasty whose talents led to rapid promotion. He promoted the assimilation of northern nomad tribes to Han culture. He was ennobled for his role in the planning of the removal of the capital from Datong to Luoyang and became an imperial adviser.

Guoyu: An early historical work which takes the form of a compilation of court records and other material from the Zhou dynasty between 990 and 453 BC. Its authorship has been a matter of dispute but has been ascribed to Zuo Qiuming of the early Spring and Autumn period. Its principal characteristic is a concentration upon historical personages.

Han Fei (c.280 – 233 BC): Legalist philosopher. His collected writings (*Han Feizi*) were assembled posthumously. Some have been translated in Burton Watson (1964). *Han Fei Tzu: Basic Writings*. New York: Columbia University Press. A complete translation by W. K. Liao (London: Arthur Probsthain, 1939) is available online.

Han Ying: Poet and official of the Western Han dynasty and the originator of a poetic form to which he gave his name.

Han Yu (768 – 824): Scholar, poet, highly regarded essayist and official whose early career was somewhat chequered. He advocated centralized government and opposed the Tang dynasty system of devolved provincial governorships. As an orthodox Confucian his political views were complicated.

Hong Zicheng (1573 – 1620): Also known as Hong Yingming, a late Ming writer of whom little is known. *Vegetable Roots Discourse* (*Cai Gen Tan*) contains a section on the art of self cultivation and combines elements of Confucian, Daoist and Buddhist thought. There are many translations of this quaintly named work. The author spent some time as a hermit.

Hu Hong (1106 – 1162): Southern Song philosopher of the Rationalist School who, despite never holding an official post, devoted as much energy to matters of state as to scholarship.

Huainanzi: See *Liu An*.

Huan Kuan: Han dynasty official. The *Debates on Salt and Iron* (*Yan Tie Lun*) is his account of the proceedings of an imperial conference in 81 BC which examined the problems of the supply of salt and iron. It was the first systematic treatment of the problem.

Huang Tingjian (1045 – 1105): Poet and calligrapher of the Northern Song dynasty and founder of the Jiangxi style of poetry. He was a pupil of Su Shi (q.v.), with whom his name became associated as "Su-Huang."

Huang Zongxi (1610 – 1695): Son of a father who sought to impeach one of the court eunuchs, was imprisoned and subsequently died of ill treatment. He was praised for the way in which he sought posthumous justice for his father. Like many Qing scholars he was interested in astronomy and mathematics. His calculations, based on the occurrence of solar eclipses, cast some doubt on the previously accepted dating of major historical works.

Huangfu Shi (c.777 – c.835): Tang official and literary figure, pupil of Han Yu (q.v.).

Ji Kang (223 – 262 or 224 – 263): Author, poet, Daoist philosopher and musician of the period of the Three Kingdoms.

Ji Yun (1724 – 1805): Scholar and official. Also known as Ji Xiaolan and "Tobacco Pouch Ji" because of his addiction to tobacco. He was chief editor of the *Complete Library in Four Branches* (*Si Ku Quan Shu*) a selection of over 3,000 titles made for the imperial library, a process which began in 1771.

Jia Dao (779 – 843): Tang dynasty poet, who started life as a monk and later returned to secular life. Tradition has it that a poem of his complaining about a curfew on monks brought him to the attention of Han Yu (q.v.) with whom he subsequently studied.

Jia Yi (200 – 168 BC): Political theorist and imperial adviser (*Bo Shi*) at the age of 21. Died of grief and remorse at the age of 33 after his ruler was killed in a riding accident.

Li Ao (772 – 836): Tang dynasty philosopher, essayist and official. Pupil of Han Yu (q.v.) whom he assisted in promoting the ancient literature movement. He wrote an account of a trip to the South, *Coming to the South* (*Lai Nan Lu*) which has some claim to be one of the earliest diaries.

Li Bai (701 – 762): Famous Tang dynasty poet. A literary prodigy as a child, he was born and brought up in north-west China. He had an interest in martial arts and spent his early manhood travelling. He was employed for a while at the Hanlin Academy but was forced to leave the capital for political reasons. He later became an associate of the poet Du Fu (q.v.) in Luoyang. He was caught up in the events of the An Lushan rebellion in 756 and exiled but pardoned en route. His later life was one of some hardship. His travels gave him a sympathy for the sufferings of the people which was reflected in his poetry. His poetry has been described as filled with the spirit of romanticism.

Li Baiyao (565 – 648): Tang dynasty historian who completed the official history of Northern Qi, the *Book of Northern Qi* (*Bei Qi Shu*), started by his father Li Delin.

Li Er: Known as Laozi. One of the principal Chinese philosophers and founder of the Daoist school of philosophy of the Spring and Autumn period; author of the *Classic of Morality* (*Dao De Jing*), which describes the Dao as the mystical source and ideal of all existence: invisible, but immensely powerful; the root of all things.

Li Gang (1083 – 1140): A Song dynasty military official renowned for his resistance to the Tatar (Jin) hordes and his (largely unheeded) strategic advice.

Li Qingzhao (1084 – c.1151): Song dynasty poet and one of China's greatest women poets. Her father was a well known scholar and her early life was lived in some luxury. She and her husband (who later died) were both art collectors and were forced to flee to southern China by the troops of the invading Jin dynasty. Her early poetic style was one of elegant restraint but after the death of her husband her poetry reflected the sadness and hardships of her life.

Li Qunyu: Tang dynasty poet whose poems met with imperial approval. The short poem *Releasing Fish* (*Fang*

Yu) is regarded as having profound philosophical significance.

Li Ruzhen (c.1763 – c.1830): Qing dynasty writer and novelist. *Flowers in the Mirror* (*Jing Hua Yuan*), a novel of fantasy, rather resembles *Gulliver's Travels*, but with fairies. It is the source of the phrase "let a hundred flowers bloom" (*bai hua qi fang*).

Li Zhi (1527 – 1602): Ming dynasty scholar and official. He was imprisoned on a false accusation and later committed suicide.

Liang Qichao (1873 – 1929): Scholar and journalist, one of the leaders of the reformist movement of the late 19th and early 20th centuries. The fluency of his written style contributed to the modernization of literary forms. He was also extremely politically active but spent his later years teaching and writing.

Liang Zhangju (1775 – 1849): Qing dynasty civil and military official and writer.

Lie Yukou: Known as Liezi, Daoist philosopher of the early period of the Warring States. He advocated *qing jing wu wei*, a passive view of life which emphasized the natural order.

Lin Bu (967 – 1029): Reclusive naturist poet of the Northern Song dynasty. He lived as a hermit on Mount Gushan by Hangzhou's Western Lake where he spent time visiting temples by boat. On the arrival of guests his servant was instructed to release a crane to summon him home. He is reputed not to have visited a town for over 20 years.

Lin Zexu (1785 – 1850): Late Qing official and Viceroy of the Two Guangs (the provinces of Guangdong and Guangxi), he played a major role in resistance to western attempts to develop the opium trade through the port of Canton (Guangdong). Despatched to Canton in 1839 as Imperial Envoy with the task of suppressing the trade, he confiscated and destroyed the complete stock of opium held by British traders in their godown. Following the Opium War of 1840 he was blamed for the failure to defeat British military operations and was demoted and exiled to Xinjiang. His *Poem of Farewell to His Family* was written on the eve of his departure. He is regarded as a national hero.

Liu An (179 – 122 BC): Prince and scholar. Reputed inventor of *Doufu* (bean curd). The *Huainanzi* was a treatise which refined the essence of the Daoist philosophers before the Qin dynasty but included miscellaneous stories and legends as well as other material.

Liu E (1857 – 1909): Scholar and novelist prominent in research into the oracle bone fragments. His short satirical novel *The Travels of Lao Can* (*Lao Can You Ji*) attacked the corruption of the late Qing dynasty bureaucracy. It has been translated into English a number of times.

Liu Ji (1311 – 1375): Scholar, official and poet at the end of the Yuan dynasty and the beginning of the

Ming. In later life he took service under the Ming as a military adviser and acquired a considerable reputation as a strategist, on a level with Zhuge Liang (q.v.).

Liu Shao (c.186 – 245): Philosopher of the period of the Three Kingdoms. His *Records of People* (*Ren Wu Zhi*) related the physical characteristics of the human body to the five Chinese elements: metal, wood, water, fire and earth. It also related this spiritual metaphor to the five constant Confucian virtues: Benevolence, Righteousness, Propriety, Wisdom and Fidelity.

Liu Xiang (c.77 – 6 BC): Lexicographer and official. His *Garden of Stories* (*Shuo Yuan*) was a collection of historical stories and legends with a commentary which promoted Confucian moral and political concepts.

Liu Xie (c.465 – 532): Known as Liu Bowen, scholar and official, but best known for his literary achievements, particularly *The Literary Mind and the Carving of Dragons* (*Wen Xin Diao Long*) an early major work of literary criticism.

Liu Yuxi (772 – 842): Tang dynasty philosopher, poet and official who became one of the central figures in the political reform movement led by Wang Shuwen (753 – 806).

Liu Zhiji (661 – 721): Tang dynasty historian who wrote the first Chinese commentary on historiography.

Liu Zhou (514 – 565): Writer. In *Liuzi* he outlined his ideas for government and the nurture of talent.

Liu Zongyuan (773 – 819): Philosopher, writer and official. Left over 600 works but his reputation rested on poetry. He suffered a number of demotions during his career. A good friend of Bai Juyi (q.v.).

Lu Jia: Writer, statesman of the state of Chu. Famed for his powers of persuasion.

Lu Jiuyuan (1139 – 1193): Southern Song dynasty philosopher, educator and founder of Neo-Confucianism School of Mind (*Xin Xue*).

Lu Shanji (1575 – 1636): Of Mongolian extraction and born into a distinguished family in Hebei province. He followed an official career mainly in the Hoppo (Hubu), one of the six Boards, which was broadly responsible for finance, commerce and customs.

Lu Shiyi (1611 – 1672): Scholar of broad interests and accomplishments who devoted himself to a life of secluded study on the fall of the Ming dynasty in 1644.

Lu You (1125 – 1210): Patriotic and prolific poet (more than 9,300 poems). Forced by his mother to separate from his wife, an event which influenced the rest of his life.

Lu Zhi (754 – 805): Enlightened and outspoken official to the Emperor Dezong who advocated policies that did much to prevent the collapse of his rule.

Lü Buwei (? – 235 BC): Statesman in the state of Qin. His *Lü's Spring and Autumn Annals* (*Lü Shi Chun Qiu*) is mainly a compilation of the writings of scholars before the Qin dynasty.

Lü Desheng (fl.1521 – 1566): A Ming dynasty writer. His *Words for Children* (*Xiao Er Yu*) was an updated collection of moralistic sayings designed to inculcate good behavior.

Lü Kun (1536 – 1618): A Ming dynasty thinker and official in the Board of Punishments. He wrote several books of which *Lamentations* (*Shen Yin Yu*) is one.

Lü Zuqian (1137 – 1181): Born of an illustrious official family he was more interested in scholarship than an official career despite his outstanding performance in the imperial examinations.

Luo Dajing (1196 – 1252): Song official. Although he held a number of provincial posts as a legal official he abandoned his career and devoted himself to literary criticism after being implicated in court intrigue and impeached. *Dew of Jade in the Forest of Cranes* (*He Lin Yu Lu*) includes notes and commentaries on poets of earlier dynasties.

Meng Ke (c.372 – 289 BC): Also known as Mencius. Disciple, at two generations removed, of Confucius. He advocated benevolent government.

Mo Di (c.468 – 376 BC): Founder of the philosophical school of Mohism which emphasized universal love on the basis of equality rather than social degree. He regarded war as a malady of his times. His work *Mozi* includes a section against war.

Ouyang Xiu (1007 – 1072): Song dynasty scholar, historian, poet and upright official. Political and literary reformist.

Pei Songzhi (372 – 451): Southern Song dynasty historian.

Pi Rixiu (c.838 – c.883): Poet and official of the Tang dynasty.

Pu Songling (1640 – 1715): Short story writer and essayist of the Qing dynasty. His fame rests mostly on his collection of short stories *Liao Zhai Zhi Yi*-translated into English as *Strange Stories from a Chinese Studio* by H.A. Giles (1845 – 1935) and more recently by John Minford.

Qi Jiguang (1528 – 1587): Ming dynasty military theorist and general who, by re-thinking tactics, organization and weapons eradicated Japanese piracy in the maritime provinces of east and south-east China.

Qian Qi (1467 – 1542): Ming dynasty official and poet.

Qu Yuan (c.340 – c.278 BC): Official and statesman of the state of Chu and one of China's greatest romantic poets. *Sorrow at Parting* (*Li Sao*) is a lengthy lyric poem of political content. It expresses the poet's feelings at the suffering he has endured and criticizes the state of the nation.

Record of History (Shi Ji): See *Sima Qian*.

Record of Rites Compiled by Dai De (Da Dai Li Ji): A compilation of the sayings and opinions of Confucian scholars before the Qin and Han dynasties. Believed to have been compiled by Dai De during the Western Han dynasty.

Record of the Hall of Beauty (You Mei Tang Ji): A piece by Ouyang Xiu (q.v.) in praise of a beauty spot near Hangzhou.

Recorded Sayings of Dahui Zonggao: Record of the sayings of a Zen Buddhist monk who lived from 1089 – 1163.

Shang Yang (c.390 – 338 BC): Political philosopher and minister of the state of Qin who advocated both measures intended to strengthen the Qin state and government of remarkable harshness and cruelty. In the end, he perished equally cruelly at the hands of his enemies—he was torn limb from limb. His legalist philosophy was recorded in *The Book of Lord Shang*.

Shen Dao (c.395 – c.315 BC): Legalist philosopher who taught in the state of Qi during the period of the Warring States.

Shen Deqian (1673 – 1769): Qing dynasty scholar and poet.

Shen Hanguang (1618 – 1677): Poet who brought up his two younger brothers after the death of his father, an official under the previous (Ming) dynasty.

Shen Juyun: Qing scholar.

Shen Kuo (1031 – 1095): An official of wide scientific interests who was sensitive to environmental issues. When governor of Yanzhou (today's Yan'an in Shaanxi province) he recorded the existence of oil whilst on campaign against Xixia incursions.

Shi Jiao (c.390 – c.330 BC): Legalist philosopher of the Warring States period and author of *Shizi*.

Shi Nai'an: Author of *The Water Margin* (*Shui Hu Zhuan*), a collection of tales of derring-do based on the exploits of heroes of the past.

Sima Guang (1019 – 1086): Historian and essayist. Author of the first detailed and comprehensive Chinese historical chronology *Comprehensive Mirror to Aid in Government* (*Zi Zhi Tong Jian*). It covered 1,362 years from 403 BC during the period of the Warring States. His political views were conservative.

Sima Qian (c.145 or c. 135 BC – ?): Historian and thinker. His *Record of History* (*Shi Ji*) covered about 3,000 years of Chinese history from the time of the mythical Yellow Emperor to 87 BC.

Sima's Rules of War (**Sima Fa**): A military treatise incorporating earlier works and compiled during the middle of the period of the Warring States by command of King Wei of Qi (356 – 320 BC).

Sorrow at Parting (**Li Sao**): See *Qu Yuan*.

Stratagems of the Warring States (Zhan Guo Ce): A well known historical work. The identity of the original compilers is not clear but it is believed to have been edited into one work by Liu Xiang (q.v.) during the final years of the Western Han dynasty.

Su Shi (1037 – 1101): Son of Su Xun (q.v.) and far better known as the poet Su Dongpo. The *Record of the Hall of Thought* (*Si Tang Ji*) was written at the invitation of a friend, a writer of *ci* (one of the forms of Chinese poetry), who believed in the significance of "Think before acting" and had erected a building dedicated to the idea.

Su Xun (1009 – 1066): Literary figure of the Northern Song dynasty. Known with two of his sons as "the three Sus" (see *Su Shi* and *Su Zhe*). A prolific essayist with reformist political views.

Su Zhe (1039 – 1112): Son of Su Xun (q.v.). Brother of Su Shi (q.v.). Northern Song dynasty essayist.

Sun Wu: A successful general and military theorist in the state of Wu. A version of his military classic, *The Art of War* (*Sun Zi Bing Fa*) written on bamboo slips, together with a similar treatise by Sun Bin, was excavated from a Han dynasty tomb in Shandong province in 1972. His writings have remained influential in military circles to the present day. The earliest reliable translation into English was that of Lionel Giles published in 1910. There have been many others since. Sun Wu stands head and shoulders above other theorists.

Tan Qiao: Daoist scholar of the Five dynasties (907 – 960), who spent some time as a hermit and sought the pill for immortality. *The Book of Transformations* (*Hua Shu*) is an important Daoist text which advances a view of the cycle of creation that starts from the Void and moves through Spirit and Essence to Form and then returns to the Void.

Tao Qian (365 or 372 or 376 – 427): Also known as Tao Yuanming. Poet and essayist. After several years as a magistrate and minor official he resigned his position and retired to rural solitude. His poetry mainly concerns itself with the hermetic rural life.

The Book of Lord Shang (***Shang Jun Shu***): A compendium assembled during the period of the Warring States which contained the views of the politician and Legalist thinker Shang Yang (q.v.).

The Constancy of Laws (***Jing Fa***): A work of the Huang-Lao school, thought to date from the period of the Warring States and excavated from a Han dynasty tomb in Changsha in 1973.

The Literary Mind and the Carving of Dragons (***Wen Xin Diao Long***): See *Liu Xie*.

The School Sayings of Confucius (***Kong Zi Jia Yu***): First mentioned in the *Book of Han*, it was thought to be a collection of sayings and opinions attributed to Confucius. The earliest surviving compilation is by Wang Su (195 – 256). Various versions of it have circulated over the centuries with long running disputes about its authenticity.

The Six Secret Teachings on the Way of Strategy (Tai Gong Liu Tao or Liu Tao): Also known as *The Six Bow-cases of Duke Tai*. An early and justly famous work on warfare and strategy. It has been well known outside China since at least the 16th century when it was known in Japan, and there have been translations into Japanese, Russian, German and English. There is an English translation by Ralph D. Sawyer.

The Spring and Autumn Annals of Minister Yan Ying: A description of the sayings and actions of the statesman Yan Ying (? – 500 BC). There are various views about its authorship.

The Yellow Emperor's Classic of Internal Medicine (Huang Di Nei Jing): Also known as *The Inner Canon of Huangdi* or *the Yellow Emperor's Inner Canon*. A very early and important medical (and Daoist) text.

Vegetable Roots Discourse (Cai Gen Tan): See *Hong Zicheng*.

Wang Anshi (1021 – 1086): Political thinker, literary figure and prime minister to the Emperor Shenzong in 1070. A political reformer, he memorialized the throne in 1058 seeking an improvement to a situation of "an accumulation of poverty and weakness" and the adoption of the Legalist policy of enriching the state and strengthening military power (*Fu Guo Qiang Bing*), a slogan which was also used during the Meiji restoration in 19th century Japan.

Wang Bo (649 or 650 – 676): Well known Tang dynasty poet.

Wang Chong (27 – c.97): Philosopher and official of the Eastern Han dynasty.

Wang Da (1368 – 1644): Ming dynasty author.

Wang Fu (c.85 – 162): Philosopher of the Eastern Han dynasty. A commentator who was critical of the corruption and avarice of the court at a time of social instability and natural disaster. The *Discourse of a Man Concealed* (*Qian Fu Lun*) was an acerbic political polemic written by a man who never sought office and lived in seclusion. Some passages in the book are still regarded as obscure.

Wang Fuzhi (1619 – 1692): Great scholar of the last years of the Ming dynasty. He took part in resistance to the Qing dynasty. In philosophy he summarized and developed the traditional Chinese theory of materialism—that matter precedes spirit.

Wang Tingxiang (1474 – 1544): Scholar and independent thinker who opposed rigid adherence to old forms merely for the sake of them. He had an interest in the natural sciences, especially astronomy and geography. He eventually achieved high office as Secretary of the Military Board in Nanjing.

Wang Tong (584 – 617): Philosopher and official who set up a private academy of more than one thousand disciples. *True Sayings* (*Zhong Shuo*) collects Wang's teaching and observations on the model of the *Analects of Confucius*.

Wang Yangming (1472 – 1529): Original name Wang Shouren. The name Yangming derived from his hometown Yangming Cave. Ming dynasty scholar, philosopher, educator and civil and military official. Raised severely by his parents who, angered by their son's reluctance to study and his addiction to chess, threw his chess set into a river. The son's response was this poem:

> *The chess set that was joy in passing days,*
> *By mother cruelly tossed away.*
> *Soldiers, pawns unsaved from the river flood,*
> *Generals in formation drowned.*
> *Torrent driven horses surge a thousand li,*
> *Elephants downstream amid the river's wave.*
> *The world trembles at the cannon's sound,*
> *Zhuge Liang the sleeping dragon now awakes.*

Wang subsequently modelled himself on Zhuge Liang (q.v.), the famous general and strategist and went on to suppress anti-dynastic peasant risings in south east and central south China. The influence of his philosophical teachings based on the Neo-Confucianism School of Mind (*Xin Xue*) reached beyond China to Japan and Korea.

Wang Bi (226 –249): Wei dynasty scholar of the period of the Three Kingdoms who belonged to a school of metaphysics which combined elements of Confucian and Daoist thought. Amongst his many works, the most well known are the *Commentary on Laozi* (*Lao Zi Zhu*) and *Commentary on the Book of Changes* (*Zhou Yi Zhu*).

Wang Wei (701? – 761): Poet, artist and musician. Known as the Buddha of poetry. Deeply influenced by the Zen School of Buddhism.

Wei Liaozi: A text on military strategy written by Wei Liao. One of the military classics of ancient China.

Wei Yingwu (c.737 – c.791): Tang dynasty naturist poet who also followed an official career. His poetry reflected a hankering after the pastoral life.

Wei Zheng (580 – 643): An Imperial Censor under the Tang dynasty. An orthodox Confucian who believed in the Confucian virtues rather than the efficacy of severe punishment as a means of government.

Wu Jing (669 or 670 – 749): Tang dynasty historian and official. *Outline of Affairs during the Zhenguan Reign of the Tang Dynasty* (*Zhen Guan Zheng Yao*) is a major source of material on imperial and ministerial conversations, memorials and prescripts in the period of the Tang emperor Taizong (599 – 649).

Wu Qi (? – 381 BC): Military theorist on a par with Sun Wu. *Wuzi* is the only surviving part of a longer *Wuqi* written in the early Warring States period. *Wuzi* developed Sun Wu's principles of war.

Xu Gan (171 – 218): Poet, philosopher and literary

figure of the Eastern Han dynasty.

Xue Xuan (1389 or 1392 – 1464): Neo-Confucianist scholar and official who followed in the footsteps of Zhu Xi (q.v.).

Xun Kuang (c.313 – 238 BC): Known as Xunzi. Thinker, educator and literary figure of the state of Zhao. He travelled widely and criticized and developed the ideas of the pre-Qin philosophers on the basis of his own Confucian views. He did not share Meng Ke's (q.v.) view that humanity was basically virtuous and believed that the natural order proceeded under its own momentum and not at the behest of man.

Xun Yue (148 – 209): Easter Han dynasty philosopher and historian from a poor family who could memorize at sight and was able to recite and explain the *Spring and Autumn Annals* as a child. *The Mirror of History* (*Shen Jian*) attacked the use of divination to form policy and advocated a number of other reforms.

Yan Yanzhi (384 – 456): Literary figure, poet and official with service as an infantry officer. A close friend of Tao Qian (q.v.). Some critics regard his poetry as rather artificial and a little lifeless.

Yan Yuan (1635 – 1704): Educational theorist who criticized established educational practice. He believed in the paramount importance of fostering talent.

Yan Zhenqing (708 – 784): Official and noted calligrapher whose life came to an end when he was strangled by a rebellious general. Two years later the general was murdered by his own subordinates and the rebellion came to an end.

Yan Zhitui (531 – after c.590): Official. His educational views, which were Confucian, were influential. *The Family Instructions of Master Yan* (*Yan Shi Jia Xun*) was the first comprehensive and systematic educational manual in China. Based on Yan's personal experience its scope extended beyond family education to history, literature and ethics. His personal life was eventful.

Yan Zun: A hermetic scholar of the Western Han dynasty who refused official preferment and earned his living by divination. Once he had earned enough for his daily needs he returned to his study of Laozi.

Yang Shi (1053 – 1135): Philosopher, scholar and pupil of Cheng Hao and Cheng Yi (q.v.).

Yang Wanli (1127 – 1206): Scholar, official and poet. Frequently memorialized the throne on topics such as the needs of defense.

Yang Xiong (53 BC – 18 AD): Poet, linguist and scholar who overcame the disability of a stammer to win imperial favor on the basis of his poetic gifts. He wrote the first Chinese lexicon of dialects.

Yao Chong (650 – 721): Tang dynasty official who served as Prime Minister under three reigns—Wu Zetian, her son Emperor Ruizong, and her grandson Emperor Xuanzong.

Ye Mengde (1077 – 1148): Song dynasty poet. He pursued a career as an official and lived as a hermit in his later years.

Yuan Cai (? – 1195): Scholar, official and gazetteer, his only surviving work is *Yuan's Hereditary Rules* (*Yuan Shi Shi Fan*) on family morality and relationships.

Yuan Mei (1716 – 1798): Successful provincial official and poet and essayist with a large following. Resigned his position at the age of 33 (or 40) in order to look after his widowed mother. He restored a dilapidated property in Nanjing and lived there for nearly 50 years. Apart from poetry he also wrote two popular collections of tales of the fantastic and a cookery book published in 1792.

Yuan Zhen (779 – 831): Tang dynasty poet and official. He was an associate of Bai Juyi (q.v.) with whom he advocated the adoption of a new poetic form first proposed at the beginning of the Tang dynasty by the poet Du Fu (q.v.).

Yue Ke (1183 – c.1242): Song dynasty scholar and official. The *Court Tales* (*Ting Shi*) is an account of the activities within and without the Northern and Southern Song court. Its style is close to that of a novel.

Zeng Guofan (1811 – 1872): Controversial late Qing dynasty statesman, minister and military figure. In 1853 he raised an army in his home province of Hunan and took the field against the rebels of the Taiping Movement, basically a peasant rising which was suppressed over the next ten years. *Letters of Zeng Guofan to His Family* (*Zeng Wen Zheng Gong Jia Shu*) on the proper conduct of households, appeared after his death and is more a manual of behavior than a guide to domestic administration.

Zhang Jiuling (673 or 678 – 740): Scholar, official and poet of the Tang dynasty.

Zhang Shunmin: Northern Song dynasty official and poet.

Zhang Xuecheng (1738 – 1801): Thinker, historian and historical critic with a particular interest in local histories and historical methodology.

Zhang Zai (1020 – 1077): Northern Song dynasty philosopher and one of the founders of the Neo-Confucian rationalistic School of Principle (*Li Xue*). His texts were required reading for candidates in the imperial examinations during the Ming and Qing dynasties.

Zhao Chongguo (137 – 52 BC): Western Han dynasty archer, cavalryman and general. Active in the North West in campaigns against the Xiongnu. *On the Twelve Advantages of Military Farms* (*Tiao Shang Tun Tian Bian Yi Shi Er Shi Zhuang*) emphasized the function of garrisons in stabilizing areas occupied by nomadic tribes thus avoiding the expense of maintaining an army in the field.

Zheng Xie (1693 – 1765): Artist, calligrapher and poet.

Either side of an official career he lived in Yangzhou. One of the Eight Masters of Yangzhou.

Zhou Shouchang (1814 – 1884): Qing dynasty scholar, official and poet who played a prominent part in the actions to suppress the Taiping Rebellion of 1851 – 1864.

Zhou Xingsi (469 – 521): Official and courtier. The *Thousand Character Classic* (*Qian Zi Wen*) contains 1,000 characters in groups of four which describe nature and the life of man without using each character more than once. There is, in fact, one repetition so there are actually only 999 characters. Tradition has it that the text was written overnight at the command of the emperor and that by morning the author's hair had turned white.

Zhu Bailu (1617 – 1688): Qing dynasty educator.

Zhu Shunshui (1600 – 1682): Alternative name of Zhu Ziyu. Civil and military official and philosopher in the latter years of the Ming dynasty who took part in resistance activities against the incoming Qing dynasty. On the final collapse of the Ming he fled to Japan and then to Annam. Despite the stringent regulations prohibiting the entry of foreigners, the Japanese scholar Ando Seian (1622 – 1701) was later able to secure a living for him in Nagasaki and Edo (later Tokyo) where he taught for more than 20 years. His Neo-Confucian philosophical teachings had considerable influence in Japan.

Zhu Xi (1130 – 1200): Southern Song dynasty Confucian scholar, educator and founder of the school of Neo-Confucianism.

Zhuang Zhou (c.369 – 286 BC): Also known as Zhuangzi. Early Daoist philosopher of the Warring States period.

Zhuge Liang (181 – 234): Famous strategist, general, statesman and inventor of the period of the Three Kingdoms. Zhuge Liang believed that there were nine qualities required of a successful general and eight faults to be avoided. He invented the wheelbarrow and remains a central character of Chinese historical films.

Zuo Qiuming: Or Zuoqiu Ming. Historian of the Spring and Autumn period in the state of Lu. His chronicle of events *Chronicle of Zuo* (*Zuo Zhuan*) covers the period c.722 – 464 BC.

Zuo Si (c.250 – c.305): Poet of the Western Jin dynasty. Of unprepossessing appearance and by nature retiring he moved to court when his younger sister was taken into court. He was active in literary circles.

Dynasties in Chinese History

Xia dynasty	2070 BC – 1600 BC
Shang dynasty	1600 – 1046 BC
Zhou dynasty	1046 – 256 BC
Western Zhou dynasty	1046 – 771 BC
Eastern Zhou dynasty	770 – 256 BC
Spring and Autumn period	770 – 476 BC
Warring States period	475 – 221 BC
Qin dynasty	221 BC – 206 BC
Han dynasty	206 BC – AD 220
Western Han dynasty	206 BC – AD 25
Eastern Han dynasty	25 – 220
Three Kingdoms	220 – 280
Wei	220 – 265
Shu Han	221 – 263
Wu	222 – 280
Jin dynasty	265 – 420
Western Jin dynasty	265 – 316
Eastern Jin dynasty	317 – 420
Northern and Southern dynasties	420 – 589
Southern dynasties	420 – 589
Northern dynasties	439 – 581
Sui dynasty	581 – 618
Tang dynasty	618 – 907
Five dynasties and Ten States	907 – 960
Five dynasties	907 – 960
Ten States	902 – 979
Song dynasty	960 – 1279
Northern Song dynasty	960 – 1127
Southern Song dynasty	1127 – 1279
Liao dynasty	916 – 1125
Jin dynasty	1115 – 1234
Xixia dynasty	1038 – 1227
Yuan dynasty	1279 – 1368
Ming dynasty	1368 – 1644
Qing dynasty	1644 – 1911